GW00356703

This journal belongs to:

....

....

Introduction

Q&A Journal for Kids provides a unique opportunity to sit down with your kids and document how they are growing and changing before your eyes. With this tool, you will be able to ask your kids a question each day for the next three years. This little book will serve your family well as a place to meet together daily to talk about both the silly and the serious and then document it along the way. Together you and your kids will be able to visit the same question on the same day year after year and watch how your child's thoughts about life and the world change. Each question is also partnered with an encouraging verse from the Bible that will help point your family to what the Word of God says about the serious and the funny. This daily exercise allows you to see how your child is taking in the world and gives you an opportunity to coach them through tough topics.

What a treat it will be for your kids to read their thoughts from when they were small. You are modeling and training them to ask hard questions, be true to themselves, the invaluable practice of journaling. This daily practice will help them know themselves better as well as teach them about what God's Word in the Bible has to say about daily life. What a treasure it will be to have this season written down to be able to re-visit again and again.

FREELY GIVE CO.

Unless otherwise indicated, all Scripture quotations are taken from the Holy Bible, *New International Version,* ® NIV. ® Copyright© 1973, 1978, 1984, 2011 by Biblica, Inc.® Used by permission. All rights reserved worldwide.

Copyright © 2017 by Freely Give Co.
Written by Scott Bowen
Cover Design by Annabelle Grobler

www.freelygive.com

ISBN: 978-0-9976368-8-8

Printed in China

January

What is the best thing about you?

20__ _____

_____

_____

_____

20__ _____

_____

_____

_____

20__ _____

_____

_____

_____

"I have been crucified with Christ and I no longer live, but Christ lives in me. The life I now live in the body, I live by faith in the Son of God, who loved me and gave himself for me."

Galatians 2:20

January

2

What would you buy if money really did grow on trees?

20__ _____

_____

_____

_____

20__ _____

_____

_____

_____

20__ _____

_____

_____

_____

"Do not store up for yourselves treasures on earth, where moth and rust destroy, and where thieves break in and steal."

Matthew 6:19

January

Why is your heart sad when friends are mean?

20__ _____

_____

_____

_____

20__ _____

_____

_____

_____

20__ _____

_____

_____

_____

"Be kind and compassionate to one another, forgiving each other."

Ephesians 4:32

January

What do you think you will look like in 20 years?

20__ _____

20__ _____

20__ _____

"For I know the plans I have for you," declares the LORD, "plans to prosper you and not to harm you, plans to give you hope and a future."

Jeremiah 29:11

January

5

Who will be the hero of your life?

20__ _____

_____

_____

_____

20__ _____

_____

_____

_____

20__ _____

_____

_____

_____

"For God did not send his Son into the world to condemn the world, but to save the world through him."

John 3:17

January

Do you think you will ever have a friend on another continent?

20__ _____

_____

_____

_____

20__ _____

_____

_____

_____

20__ _____

_____

_____

_____

"Abraham believed God, and it was credited to him as righteousness," and he was called God's friend.

James 2:23

January

20__ _____

_____

_____

_____

20__ _____

_____

_____

_____

20__ _____

_____

_____

_____

"He was looking forward to the city with foundations, whose architect and builder is God."

Hebrews 11:10

January Is heaven a real place?

20__ _____

_____

_____

_____

20__ _____

_____

_____

_____

20__ _____

_____

_____

_____

"In the beginning God created the heavens and the earth."

Genesis 1:1

January

What is one thing you would change if you were president?

20__ _____

_____

_____

_____

20__ _____

_____

_____

_____

20__ _____

_____

_____

_____

"I urge, then, first of all, that petitions, prayers, intercession and thanksgiving be made for all people – for kings and all those in authority, that we may live peaceful and quiet lives in all godliness and holiness."

1 Timothy 2:1-2

January

10

How would your
life change if
you never made
a bad choice?

20__ _____

_____

_____

_____

20__ _____

_____

_____

_____

20__ _____

_____

_____

_____

"And we know that in all things God works
for the good of those who love him, who
have been called according to his purpose."

Romans 8:28

January

11

How would your life change if you would never tell a lie?

20__ _____

_____

_____

_____

20__ _____

_____

_____

_____

20__ _____

_____

_____

_____

"Yet you desired faithfulness even
in the womb; you taught me
wisdom in that secret place."

Psalm 51:6

January

12

What would life
be like if you
were famous?

20__ _____

_____

_____

_____

20__ _____

_____

_____

_____

20__ _____

_____

_____

_____

"Many are the plans in a human
heart, but it is the LORD's
purpose that prevails."

Proverbs 19:21

January What would happen if your greatest fear came true?

20__ _____

_____

_____

_____

20__ _____

_____

_____

_____

20__ _____

_____

_____

_____

"There is no fear in love. But perfect love drives out fear."

1 John 4:18

January

 **14**

What would happen
if your greatest
dream came true?

20__ _____

_____

_____

_____

20__ _____

_____

_____

_____

20__ _____

_____

_____

_____

"But seek first his kingdom and his
righteousness, and all these things
will be given to you as well."

Matthew 6:33

January  What things would you do if you were never embarrassed?

20__ _____

_____

_____

_____

20__ _____

_____

_____

_____

20__ _____

_____

_____

_____

"For all those who exalt themselves will be humbled, and those who humble themselves will be exalted."

Luke 14:11

January

16

What is the first thing you would do if you were the one to discover the new world?

20__ _____

_____

_____

_____

20__ _____

_____

_____

_____

20__ _____

_____

_____

_____

"Call to me and I will answer you and tell you great and unsearchable things you do not know."

Jeremiah 33:3

January

What would you do if you were never afraid?

20__ _____

_____

_____

_____

20__ _____

_____

_____

_____

20__ _____

_____

_____

_____

"He will cover you with his feathers, and under his wings you will find refuge."

Psalm 91:4

January

18

Why do you think people are different colors?

20__ _____

_____

_____

_____

20__ _____

_____

_____

_____

20__ _____

_____

_____

_____

"From one man he made all the nations, that they should inhabit the whole earth."

Acts 17:26

January

19 Why do you think people don't always agree with you?

20__ _____

_____

_____

_____

20__ _____

_____

_____

_____

20__ _____

_____

_____

_____

"Accept those whose faith is weak, without quarreling over disputable matters."

Romans 14:1

January

Why do bad choices sometimes seem better than good choices?

20__ _____

_____

_____

_____

20__ _____

_____

_____

_____

20__ _____

_____

_____

_____

"When the woman saw that the fruit of the tree was good for food and pleasing to the eye, and also desirable for gaining wisdom, she took some and ate it. She also gave some to her husband, who was with her, and he ate it."

Genesis 3:6

January

21 Is the earth the only planet with life?

20__ _____

_____

_____

_____

20__ _____

_____

_____

_____

20__ _____

_____

_____

_____

"For in him all things were created: things in heaven and on earth."

Colossians 1:16

January

Why are people willing to die for what they believe?

20__ _____

_____

_____

_____

20__ _____

_____

_____

_____

20__ _____

_____

_____

_____

"I face death every day - yes, just as surely as I boast about you in Christ Jesus our Lord."

1 Corinthians 15:31

January

What would motivate you to cheat on a test?

20__ _____

_____

_____

_____

20__ _____

_____

_____

_____

20__ _____

_____

_____

_____

"The integrity of the upright guides them."

Proverbs 11:3

January

24

What is your favorite childhood memory?

20__ _____

_____

_____

_____

20__ _____

_____

_____

_____

20__ _____

_____

_____

_____

"I think it is right to refresh your memory as long as I live in the tent of this body."

2 Peter 1:13

January

What would it be like if you didn't have a home to come to?

20__ _____

_____

_____

_____

20__ _____

_____

_____

_____

20__ _____

_____

_____

_____

"And my God will meet all your needs."

Philippians 4:19

January

26

After you die, how will people say your life influenced them?

20__ _____

_____

_____

_____

20__ _____

_____

_____

_____

20__ _____

_____

_____

_____

"What does the Lord require of you? To act justly and to love mercy and to walk humbly with your God."

Micah 6:8

January

27 — What kind of person do you think you will marry?

20__ _____

_____

_____

_____

20__ _____

_____

_____

_____

20__ _____

_____

_____

_____

"So give your servant a discerning heart."

1 Kings 3:9

January

28 What would your life be like without social media?

20__ _____

_____

_____

_____

20__ _____

_____

_____

_____

20__ _____

_____

_____

_____

"May these words of my mouth and this meditation of my heart be pleasing in your sight, Lord, my Rock and my Redeemer."

Psalm 19:14

January

 29

What professional sport would you like to play?

20__ _____

_____

_____

_____

20__ _____

_____

_____

_____

20__ _____

_____

_____

_____

"Everyone who competes in the games goes into strict training."

1 Corinthians 9:25

January

30

Why does it feel good to give to others in need?

20__ _____

_____

_____

_____

20__ _____

_____

_____

_____

20__ _____

_____

_____

_____

"It is more blessed to give than to receive."

Acts 20:35

January

31

Why do you think we often hurt the people who are closest to us?

20__ _____

_____

_____

_____

20__ _____

_____

_____

_____

20__ _____

_____

_____

_____

"Get rid of all bitterness, rage and anger, brawling and slander."

Ephesians 4:31

February

1

Why do you think we are sometimes unhappy with the way we were made?

20__ _____

_____

_____

_____

20__ _____

_____

_____

_____

20__ _____

_____

_____

_____

"I praise you because I am fearfully and wonderfully made."

Psalm 139:14

February 2

What superhero
would you
like to be?

20__ _____

_____

_____

_____

20__ _____

_____

_____

20__ _____

_____

_____

_____

"Though you have not seen him, you love
him; and even though you do not see him
now, you believe in him and are filled with
an inexpressible and glorious joy."

1 Peter 1:8

February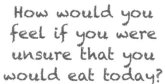

How would you feel if you were unsure that you would eat today?

20__ _____

_____

_____

_____

20__ _____

_____

_____

_____

20__ _____

_____

_____

_____

"Therefore I tell you, do not worry about your life, what you will eat or drink; or about your body, what you will wear. Is not life more important than food, and the body more important than clothes?"

Matthew 6:25

February

4

What qualities do you really admire in your best friend?

20__ _____

_____

_____

_____

20__ _____

_____

_____

_____

20__ _____

_____

_____

_____

"A friend loves at all times"

Proverbs 17:17

February

If you were given three wishes, what would they be?

20__ _____

_____

_____

_____

20__ _____

_____

_____

_____

20__ _____

_____

_____

_____

"If you remain in me and my words remain in you, ask whatever you wish, and it will be done for you."

John 15:7

February

What cheers you up when you are sad?

20__ _____

_____

_____

_____

20__ _____

_____

_____

_____

20__ _____

_____

_____

_____

"Sing and make music from
your heart to the Lord."

Ephesians 5:19

February

7

What is one thing you would change about yourself?

20__ _____

_____

_____

_____

20__ _____

_____

_____

_____

20__ _____

_____

_____

_____

"Search me, God, and know my heart."

Psalm 139:23

February

If you could design your own house, what would it look like?

20__ _____

_____

_____

_____

20__ _____

_____

_____

_____

20__ _____

_____

_____

_____

"By wisdom a house is built, and through understanding it is established."

Proverbs: 24:3

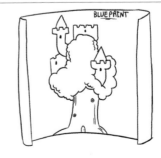

February

9

What is one thing you will never do when disciplining your kids?

20__ _____

_____

_____

_____

20__ _____

_____

_____

_____

20__ _____

_____

_____

_____

"Fathers, do not exasperate your children;
instead, bring them up in the training
and instruction of the Lord."

Ephesians 6:4

February

What is one thing you will always do when disciplining your kids?

20__ _____

_____

_____

_____

20__ _____

_____

_____

_____

20__ _____

_____

_____

_____

"Those who spare the rod hate their children, but those who love them are careful to discipline them."

Proverbs 13:24

February .oo 11

What is your favorite family memory from the last month?

20__ _____
_____
_____
_____

20__ _____
_____
_____
_____

20__ _____
_____
_____
_____

Remember the former things, those of long ago; I am God, and there is no other; I am God, and there is none like me."

Isaiah 46:9

February 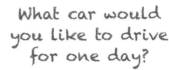 12

What car would you like to drive for one day?

20__ _____

_____

_____

_____

20__ _____

_____

_____

_____

20__ _____

_____

_____

_____

"Store up for yourselves treasures in heaven, where moths and vermin do not destroy, and where thieves do not break in and steal. 21 For where your treasure is, there your heart will be also."

Matthew 6:19-21

February

13

At what age do you think you will fall in love?

20__ _____

_____

_____

_____

20__ _____

_____

_____

_____

20__ _____

_____

_____

_____

"A wife of noble character who can find? She is worth far more than rubies."

Proverbs 31:10

February 14

What is beyond the galaxy?

20__ _____

_____

_____

_____

20__ _____

_____

_____

_____

20__ _____

_____

_____

_____

"I consider your heavens, the work of your fingers, the moon and the stars, which you have set in place."

Psalm 8:3

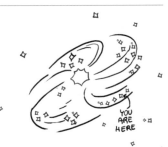

February 15

What is the nicest thing you can do for someone else?

20__ _____

_____

_____

_____

20__ _____

_____

_____

_____

20__ _____

_____

_____

_____

"Let your light shine before others, that they may see your good deeds and glorify your Father in heaven."

Matthew 5:16

February 16

Why does divorce stink?

20__ _____

_____

_____

_____

20__ _____

_____

_____

_____

20__ _____

_____

_____

_____

"Weeping may stay for the night, but re-
joicing comes in the morning."

Psalm 30:5

February

Why are there so many bad stories on the nightly news?

20__ _____

_____

_____

_____

20__ _____

_____

_____

_____

20__ _____

_____

_____

_____

"Preserve my life according to your word."

Psalm 119:25

February ···18

What would your life be like without a TV?

20__ _____

_____

_____

_____

20__ _____

_____

_____

_____

20__ _____

_____

_____

_____

"Do not love the world or anything in the world."

1 John 2:15

February

19

What career will give you the most time to be with your family?

20__ _____

_____

_____

_____

20__ _____

_____

_____

20__ _____

_____

_____

Trust in the Lord with all your heart and lean not on your own understanding; in all your ways submit to him, and he will make your paths straight."

Proverbs 3:5-6

February · °° 20

20__ _____

_____

_____

_____

20__ _____

_____

_____

_____

20__ _____

_____

_____

_____

"And we know that in all things God works for the good of those who love him."

Romans 8:28

February

21 Why are some kids popular in school and others are not?

20__ _____

_____

_____

_____

20__ _____

_____

_____

_____

20__ _____

_____

_____

_____

"Teach me to do your will, for you are my God; may your good Spirit lead me on level ground."

Psalm 143:10

February At what age will you get married?

20__ _____

_____

_____

_____

20__ _____

_____

_____

_____

20__ _____

_____

_____

_____

Do not forsake wisdom, and she will
protect you; love her, and she will
watch over you."

Proverbs 4:6

February · 23

What would it
be like if you
could fly?

20__ _____

_____

_____

_____

20__ _____

_____

_____

_____

20__ _____

_____

_____

_____

"But those who hope in the LORD will
renew their strength. They will soar
on wings like eagles; they will run
and not grow weary, they will walk
and not be faint."

Isaiah 40:31

February ..°24

What would it feel like to be a lost dog?

20__ _____

_____

_____

_____

20__ _____

_____

_____

_____

20__ _____

_____

_____

_____

"For the Son of Man came to seek
and to save what was lost."

Luke 19:10

February

 25 If it were freaky friday, who would you want to swap places with?

20__ _____

_____

_____

_____

20__ _____

_____

_____

_____

20__ _____

_____

_____

_____

"Everyone who is called by my name, whom I created for my glory, whom I formed and made."

Isaiah 43:7

February ∘∘ 26

Would you tell on a friend if he or she stole something?

20__ _____

_____

_____

_____

20__ _____

_____

_____

_____

20__ _____

_____

_____

_____

"Speaking the truth in love, we will grow to become in every respect the mature body of him who is the head, that is, Christ."

Ephesians 4:15

February 27

What is your purpose on this earth?

20__ _____
_____
_____
_____

20__ _____
_____
_____
_____

20__ _____
_____
_____
_____

"Before I formed you in the womb I knew you, before you were born I set you apart."

Jeremiah 1:5

February 28

Where will you go to college?

20__ _____

_____

_____

_____

20__ _____

_____

_____

_____

20__ _____

_____

_____

_____

"In their hearts humans plan their course,
but the Lord establishes their steps."

Proverbs 16:9

February

29 What is the best way to be friends with people who have different opinions?

20__ _____

_____

_____

_____

20__ _____

_____

_____

_____

20__ _____

_____

_____

_____

"Everyone should be quick to listen, slow to speak and slow to become angry."

James 1:19

March

1

Why is it hard to admit when you are wrong?

20__ _____

_____

_____

_____

20__ _____

_____

_____

_____

20__ _____

_____

_____

_____

"Speak truthfully to your neighbor, for we are all members of one body."

Ephesians 4:25

March

What are you REALLY good at?

20__ _____

_____

_____

_____

20__ _____

_____

_____

_____

20__ _____

_____

_____

_____

"Each of you should use whatever gift
you have received to serve others."

1 Peter 4:10

March  3

Why is it hard to apologize?

20__ _____

_____

_____

_____

20__ _____

_____

_____

_____

20__ _____

_____

_____

_____

"Confess your sins to each other and pray for each other so that you may be healed."

James 5:16

March  4

What makes your
parents proud of you?

20__ _____
_____
_____
_____
_____

20__ _____
_____
_____
_____
_____

20__ _____
_____
_____
_____
_____

"May your father and
mother rejoice."

Proverbs 23:25

March 5

Which celebrity would you love to meet?

20__ _____

_____

_____

_____

20__ _____

_____

_____

_____

20__ _____

_____

_____

_____

"I am the LORD; that is my name! I will not yield my glory to another or my praise to idols."

Isaiah 42:8

March · 6

Which bad habit will you learn from your mom?

20__ _____

_____

_____

_____

20__ _____

_____

_____

_____

20__ _____

_____

_____

_____

"She speaks with wisdom, and faithful instruction is on her tongue."

Proverbs 31:26

March

Which bad habit will you learn from your dad?

20__ _____

_____

_____

_____

20__ _____

_____

_____

_____

20__ _____

_____

_____

_____

"Perseverance, character;
and character, hope."

Romans 5:4

March

How would you act if you were able to meet your sports hero?

20__ _____

_____

_____

_____

20__ _____

_____

_____

_____

20__ _____

_____

_____

_____

"Dear children, keep yourselves from idols."

1 John 5:21

March

9

How would you describe yourself to a stranger?

20__ _____

_____

_____

_____

20__ _____

_____

_____

_____

20__ _____

_____

_____

_____

"Let your conversation be always full of grace, seasoned with salt, so that you may know how to answer everyone."

Colossians 4:6

March

10

Why does your body need food and water?

20__ _____
_____
_____
_____

20__ _____
_____
_____
_____

20__ _____
_____
_____
_____

"I am the bread of life. Whoever comes to me will never go hungry, and whoever believes in me will never be thirsty."

John 6:35

March

What is the total number of friends you will have in your life?

20__ _____

_____

_____

_____

20__ _____

_____

_____

_____

20__ _____

_____

_____

_____

"The righteous choose their friends carefully."

Proverbs 12:26

March

12

How will you influence history?

20__ _____
_____
_____
_____

20__ _____
_____
_____
_____

20__ _____
_____
_____
_____

"Whoever wants to become great
among you must be your servant."

Matthew 20:26

March · 13

How much money do you need in life?

20__ _____
_____
_____
_____

20__ _____
_____
_____
_____

20__ _____
_____
_____
_____

"Keep your life free from love of money, and be content with what you have."

Hebrews 13:5

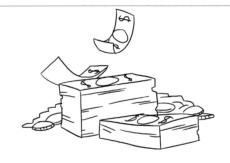

March  14

What would it be like to have a foster child staying in your home?

20__ _____

_____

_____

_____

20__ _____

_____

_____

_____

20__ _____

_____

_____

_____

"And whoever welcomes one such child in my name welcomes me."

Matthew 18:5

March  15

Would you steal
something if no one
would ever know?

20__ _____

_____

_____

_____

20__ _____

_____

_____

_____

20__ _____

_____

_____

_____

"You shall not steal."

Exodus 20:15

March 16

What will people say at your funeral?

20__ _____

_____

_____

_____

20__ _____

_____

_____

_____

20__ _____

_____

_____

_____

"Well done, good and faithful servant!"

Matthew 25:23

March  17

Why does it feel
so good to win
the big game?

20__ _____

_____

_____

_____

20__ _____

_____

_____

_____

20__ _____

_____

_____

_____

"Pride brings a person low, but
the lowly in spirit gain honor."

Proverbs 29:23

March

18

How would you react
if your best friend
offered you alcohol?

20__ _____

_____

_____

_____

20__ _____

_____

_____

_____

20__ _____

_____

_____

_____

"Walk with the wise and become wise,
for a companion of fools suffers harm."

Proverbs 13:20

March 19

How would you react if you had to move to a different state?

20__ _____

_____

_____

_____

20__ _____

_____

_____

_____

20__ _____

_____

_____

_____

"Tell the Israelites to move on."

Exodus 14:15

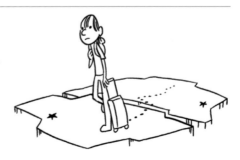

March  20

Would you ever
want to live in a
different country?

20__ _____

_____

_____

_____

20__ _____

_____

_____

_____

20__ _____

_____

_____

_____

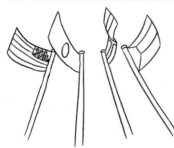

"I will instruct you and teach you in the
way you should go; I will counsel you
with my loving eye on you."

Psalm 32:8

March

21 What would be the title of your autobiography?

20__ _____

_____

_____

_____

20__ _____

_____

_____

_____

20__ _____

_____

_____

_____

"He who began a good work in you will carry it on to completion."

Philippians 1:6

March

22

Why do people let failures in their pasts ruin their futures?

20__ _____

_____

_____

_____

20__ _____

_____

_____

_____

20__ _____

_____

_____

_____

"What no eye has seen, what no ear has heard, and what no human mind has conceived the things God has prepared for those who love him."

1 Corinthians 2:9

March 23

What would it be like to lose your vision?

20__ _____

_____

_____

_____

20__ _____

_____

_____

_____

20__ _____

_____

_____

_____

"The blind and the lame came to him at the temple, and he healed them."

Matthew 21:14

March  24

What makes you really angry?

20__ _____
_____
_____
_____

20__ _____
_____
_____
_____

20__ _____
_____
_____
_____

"Do not let the sun go down while you are still angry."

Ephesians 4:26

March

What will our clothes look like in 25 years?

20__ _____

_____

_____

_____

20__ _____

_____

_____

_____

20__ _____

_____

_____

_____

"Dress modestly, with decency and propriety."

1 Timothy 2:9

March  26

What makes you really happy?

20__ _____
_____
_____
_____

20__ _____
_____
_____
_____

20__ _____
_____
_____
_____

"A happy heart makes the face cheerful."

Proverbs 15:13

March

What is the nicest thing you can say to someone?

20__ _____

_____

_____

_____

20__ _____

_____

_____

_____

20__ _____

_____

_____

_____

"Gracious words are a honeycomb, sweet to the soul and healing to the bones."

Proverbs 16:24

March  28

What makes you
cry the most?

20__ _____

_____

_____

_____

20__ _____

_____

_____

_____

20__ _____

_____

_____

_____

"He will wipe every tear from their eyes."

Revelation 21:4

March 29

What makes you scared?

20__ _____

_____

_____

_____

20__ _____

_____

_____

_____

20__ _____

_____

_____

_____

"Do not fear, for I am with you; do not
be dismayed, for I am your God. I will
strengthen you and help you; I will uphold
you with my righteous right hand."

Isaiah 41:10

March

Why do we get angry over things that don't matter?

20__ _____
_____
_____
_____

20__ _____
_____
_____
_____

20__ _____
_____
_____
_____

"Return to the LORD your God, for he is gracious and compassionate, slow to anger and abounding in love."

Joel 2:13

March 31

What would it be like if your brother or sister were famous?

20__ _____

_____

_____

_____

20__ _____

_____

_____

_____

20__ _____

_____

_____

_____

"How good and pleasant it is when brothers dwell in unity!"

Psalm 133:1 (ESV)

April

1

When are you most disgusted?

20__ _____
_____
_____
_____

20__ _____
_____
_____
_____

20__ _____
_____
_____
_____

"Do not eat any detestable thing."

Deuteronomy 14:3

April 2

What is one thing you would remove from the shelves in the supermarket?

20__ _____

_____

_____

_____

20__ _____

_____

_____

_____

20__ _____

_____

_____

_____

"Turn my eyes away from worthless things; preserve my life according to your word."

Psalm 119:37

April

3

What time period in the past would you go to if you could access time travel?

20__ _____

_____

_____

_____

20__ _____

_____

_____

_____

20__ _____

_____

_____

_____

"But do not forget this one thing, dear friends: with the Lord a day is like a thousand years, and a thousand years are like a day."

2 Peter 3:8

April

What time period in the future would you go to if you could access time travel?

20__ _____

_____

_____

_____

20__ _____

_____

_____

_____

20__ _____

_____

_____

_____

"Making the most of every opportunity, because the days are evil."

Ephesians 5:16

April 5

How old will you be when you die?

20__ _____

_____

_____

_____

20__ _____

_____

_____

_____

20__ _____

_____

_____

_____

"All the days ordained for me were written in your book."

Psalm 139:16

April 6

How many books will you read in your lifetime?

20__ _____
_____
_____
_____

20__ _____
_____
_____
_____

20__ _____
_____
_____
_____

"The heart of the discerning acquires knowledge, for the ears of the wise seek it out."

Proverbs 18:15

April 7

Is the Bible true?
How do you know?

20__ _____

_____

_____

_____

20__ _____

_____

_____

_____

20__ _____

_____

_____

_____

"Your word is a lamp for my
feet, a light on my path."

Psalm 119:105

April

What would you
do if you were
invisible for a day?

20__ _____

_____

_____

_____

20__ _____

_____

_____

_____

20__ _____

_____

_____

_____

"Then the woman, seeing that she could
not go unnoticed...fell at His feet"

Luke 8:47

April

How many sodas will you drink in your lifetime?

20__ _____
_____
_____
_____

20__ _____
_____
_____
_____

20__ _____
_____
_____
_____

"But Daniel resolved not to defile himself with the royal food."

Daniel 1:8

April 10

How tall will you be?

20__ _____
_____
_____
_____

20__ _____
_____
_____
_____

20__ _____
_____
_____
_____

"We are the clay, you are the potter;
we are all the work of your hand."

Isaiah 64:8

April

11

How many kids will you have?

20__ _____

_____

_____

_____

20__ _____

_____

_____

_____

20__ _____

_____

_____

_____

"Children are a heritage from the Lord."

Psalm 127:3

April 12

Why, at a certain age, are you embarrassed to be naked?

20__ _____
_____
_____
_____

20__ _____
_____
_____
_____

20__ _____
_____
_____
_____

"Honor God with your bodies."

1 Corinthians 6:20

April

13

Why does it feel good to hit your brother or sister?

20__ _____

_____

_____

_____

20__ _____

_____

_____

_____

20__ _____

_____

_____

_____

"Clothe yourselves with compassion, kindness, humility, gentleness and patience."

Colossians 3:12

April 14

Why do hugs feel so good?

20__ _____

_____

_____

_____

20__ _____

_____

_____

_____

20__ _____

_____

_____

_____

"Love one another with brotherly affection."

Romans 12:10 ESV

April 15

What will your life be like if you don't get an education?

20__ _____

_____

_____

_____

20__ _____

_____

_____

_____

20__ _____

_____

_____

_____

"For we are God's handiwork, created in Christ Jesus to do good works, which God prepared in advance for us to do."

Ephesians 2:10

April

16

What will be written on your tombstone?

20__ _____

_____

_____

_____

20__ _____

_____

_____

_____

20__ _____

_____

_____

_____

"But I am like an olive tree flourishing in the house of God; I trust in God's unfailing love for ever and ever."

Psalm 52:8

April 17

Does it matter if we waste things?

20__ _____
_____
_____
_____

20__ _____
_____
_____
_____

20__ _____
_____
_____
_____

"Gather the pieces that are left over. Let nothing be wasted."

John 6:12

April

 18

Which animal would you like to be for a day?

20__ _____

_____

_____

_____

20__ _____

_____

_____

_____

20__ _____

_____

_____

_____

"Look at the birds of the air; they do not sow or reap or store away in barns, and yet your heavenly Father feeds them. Are you not much more valuable than they?"

Matthew 6:26

April

19

What would it be
like to be silent
for an entire day?

20__ _____

_____

_____

_____

20__ _____

_____

_____

_____

20__ _____

_____

_____

_____

"In quietness and trust is your strength."

Isaiah 30:15

April 20

What is the weirdest thing about you?

20__ _____
_____
_____
_____

20__ _____
_____
_____
_____

20__ _____
_____
_____
_____

"You are precious and honored in my sight."

Isaiah 43:4

April 21

What would other people say is the weirdest thing about you?

20__ _____

_____

_____

_____

20__ _____

_____

_____

_____

20__ _____

_____

_____

_____

"See, I have engraved you on the palms of my hands; your walls are ever before me."

Isaiah 49:16

April 22

What would it be like to tell your sister or brother why he or she is great?

20__ _____

_____

_____

_____

20__ _____

_____

_____

_____

20__ _____

_____

_____

_____

"Therefore encourage one another and build each other up."

1 Thessalonians 5:11

April  What sounds do you hear while sleeping in a tent?

20__ _____

_____

_____

_____

20__ _____

_____

_____

_____

20__ _____

_____

_____

_____

"Let the heavens rejoice, let the earth be glad; let the sea resound, and all that is in it. Let the fields be jubilant, and everything in them; let all the trees of the forest sing for joy."

Psalm 96:11-12

April

When and where do you feel most comfortable talking to your parents?

20__ _____

_____

_____

_____

20__ _____

_____

_____

_____

20__ _____

_____

_____

_____

"We are sure that we have a clear conscience and desire to live honorably in every way."

Hebrews 13:18

April

25

Why do we hide the things we've done wrong?

20__ _____

_____

_____

20__ _____

_____

_____

20__ _____

_____

_____

"All you need to say is simply 'Yes' or 'No'."

Matthew 5:37

April 26

How do you think you are going to make a living?

20__ _____

_____

_____

_____

20__ _____

_____

_____

_____

20__ _____

_____

_____

_____

"Now he who supplies seed to the sower and bread for food will also supply and increase your store of seed and will enlarge the harvest of your righteousness."

2 Corinthians 9:10

April

27 Why do people speak different languages?

20__ _____

_____

_____

_____

20__ _____

_____

_____

_____

20__ _____

_____

_____

_____

"The Lord said, "If as one people speaking the same language they have begun to do this, then nothing they plan to do will be impossible for them. Come, let us go down and confuse their language so they will not understand each other."

Genesis 11:6-7

April What would it be like if you never cleaned your room?

20__ _____

_____

_____

_____

20__ _____

_____

_____

_____

20__ _____

_____

_____

_____

"But everything should be done in a fitting and orderly way."

1 Corinthians 14:40

April 29

What would it be like if you never brushed your teeth?

20__ _____

_____

_____

_____

20__ _____

_____

_____

_____

20__ _____

_____

_____

_____

"Blessed are those who wash their robes, that they may have the right to the tree of life and may go through the gates into the city."

Revelation 22:14

April  Why is it easier to be selfish than generous?

20__ _____

_____

_____

_____

20__ _____

_____

_____

_____

20__ _____

_____

_____

_____

"Each of you should give what you
have decided in your heart to give,
not reluctantly or under compulsion,
for God loves a cheerful giver."

2 Corinthians 9:7

May  What breaks your heart?

20__ _____

_____

_____

_____

20__ _____

_____

_____

_____

20__ _____

_____

_____

_____

"He heals the brokenhearted
and binds up their wounds."

Proverbs 147:3

May  2

What is the one
thing you are
most proud of?

20__ _____

_____

_____

_____

20__ _____

_____

_____

_____

20__ _____

_____

_____

_____

"God opposes the proud but
shows favor to the humble."

1 Peter 5:5

May

3

What two animals would you combine to make a super animal?

20__ _____

_____

_____

_____

20__ _____

_____

_____

_____

20__ _____

_____

_____

_____

"God made the wild animals according to their kinds, the livestock according to their kinds, and all the creatures that move along the ground according to their kinds. And God saw that it was good."

Genesis 1:25

May

4

If you could write a song, what would the title be?

20__ _____

_____

_____

_____

20__ _____

_____

_____

_____

20__ _____

_____

_____

_____

"He put a new song in my mouth,
a hymn of praise to our God."

Psalm 40:3

May  5

What is the most
important rule
in your house?

20__ _____

_____

_____

_____

20__ _____

_____

_____

_____

20__ _____

_____

_____

_____

"If you are willing and obedient, you
will eat the best from the land."

Isaiah 1:19

May  6

Why are things okay for your parents to say but not okay for you to say?

20__ _____

_____

_____

_____

20__ _____

_____

_____

_____

20__ _____

_____

_____

_____

"Do not let any unwholesome talk come out of your mouths."

Ephesians 4:29

May  7

What would it be like to lose your hearing?

20__ _____

_____

_____

_____

20__ _____

_____

_____

_____

20__ _____

_____

_____

_____

"This is why I speak to them in parables:
"Though seeing, they do not see; though
hearing, they do not hear or understand."

Matthew 13:13

May

8

What would you say if the whole world had to listen to you for 30 seconds?

20__ _____

_____

_____

_____

20__ _____

_____

_____

_____

20__ _____

_____

_____

_____

"God opposes the proud, but gives grace to the humble."

James 4:6

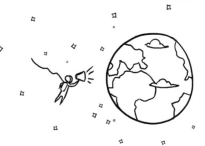

May

What will make you happy when you are 20?

20__ _____

_____

_____

_____

20__ _____

_____

_____

_____

20__ _____

_____

_____

_____

"Who satisfies your desires with good things so that your youth is renewed like the eagle's."

Psalm 103:5

May  10

What will make you happy when you are 40?

20__ _____

_____

_____

_____

20__ _____

_____

_____

_____

20__ _____

_____

_____

_____

"Dwell in the land and
enjoy safe pasture."

Psalm 37:3

May

11

What will make you happy when you are 60?

20__ _____

_____

_____

_____

20__ _____

_____

_____

_____

20__ _____

_____

_____

_____

*"Blessed are those who find wisdom,
those who gain understanding."*

Proverbs 3:13

May

12

What would life be like if people didn't have consequences to their actions?

20__ _____

_____

_____

_____

20__ _____

_____

_____

_____

20__ _____

_____

_____

_____

"Do not be deceived: God cannot be mocked. People reap what they sow."

Galatians 6:7

May

13

What changes would you make in your life if you knew you had 24 hours to live?

20__ _____

_____

_____

_____

20__ _____

_____

_____

_____

20__ _____

_____

_____

_____

"Teach us to number our days, that we may gain a heart of wisdom."

Psalm 90:12

May  14

What two words describe you best?

20__ _____

_____

_____

_____

20__ _____

_____

_____

_____

20__ _____

_____

_____

_____

"Be like-minded, be sympathetic, love one another, be compassionate and humble."

1 Peter 3:8

May  15

What will matter most to you when you are 90 years old?

20__ _____

_____

_____

_____

20__ _____

_____

_____

_____

20__ _____

_____

_____

_____

"He will renew your life and sustain you in your old age."

Ruth 4:15

May  16

How would your mom
feel if you gave her
a hug every day?

20__ _____

_____

_____

_____

20__ _____

_____

_____

_____

20__ _____

_____

_____

_____

"Her children arise and call her blessed."

Proverbs 31:28

May

17

How would your dad feel if you texted him an "I love you :-)" every day?

20__ _____

_____

_____

_____

20__ _____

_____

_____

_____

20__ _____

_____

_____

_____

"A man who fathers a wise son rejoices in him."

Proverbs 23:24

May  18

What would you
try if you knew
you would not fail?

20__ _____

_____

_____

_____

20__ _____

_____

_____

_____

20__ _____

_____

_____

_____

"Commit to the LORD whatever you do,
and he will establish your plans."

Proverbs 16:3

May

What can you teach someone else?

20__ _____

_____

_____

_____

20__ _____

_____

_____

_____

20__ _____

_____

_____

_____

"Stop judging by mere appearances."

John 7:24

May

20

What is the best thing your mom can do for you?

20__ _____

_____

_____

_____

20__ _____

_____

_____

_____

20__ _____

_____

_____

_____

"Start children off on the way they should go, and even when they are old they will not turn from it."

Proverbs 22:6

May 21

What is the best thing your dad can do for you?

20__ _____
_____
_____
_____

20__ _____
_____
_____
_____

20__ _____
_____
_____
_____

"And the one the Lord loves rests between his shoulders."

Deuteronomy 33:12

May  22

Will you live with your parents after college?

20__ _____

_____

_____

_____

20__ _____

_____

_____

_____

20__ _____

_____

_____

_____

"Therefore do not worry about tomorrow, for
tomorrow will worry about itself."

Matthew 6:34

May

23

Why do we collect things that will eventually end up in the trash?

20__ _____

_____

_____

_____

20__ _____

_____

_____

_____

20__ _____

_____

_____

_____

"Be on your guard against all kinds of greed; life does not consist in an abundance of possessions."

Luke 12:15

May  How far could you walk?

20__ _____

_____

_____

_____

20__ _____

_____

_____

_____

20__ _____

_____

_____

_____

"Go, walk through the
length and breadth
of the land, for I am
giving it to you."

Genesis 13:17

May  25

Is it possible to learn from our mistakes?

20__ _____

_____

_____

_____

20__ _____

_____

_____

_____

20__ _____

_____

_____

_____

"Those whom I love I rebuke and discipline.
So be earnest and repent."

Revelation 3:19

May  26

Is it possible to learn from our successes?

20__ _____

_____

_____

_____

20__ _____

_____

_____

_____

20__ _____

_____

_____

_____

"I can do all this through him who gives me strength."

Philippians 4:13

May  27

How many languages can you learn?

20__ _____

_____

_____

_____

20__ _____

_____

_____

_____

20__ _____

_____

_____

_____

"Undoubtedly there are all sorts of languages in the world, yet none of them is without meaning."

1 Corinthians 14:10

May  28

How would the world be different if money was never invented?

20__ _____

_____

_____

_____

20__ _____

_____

_____

_____

20__ _____

_____

_____

_____

"For the love of money is a root of all kinds of evil. Some people, eager for money, have wandered from the faith and pierced themselves with many griefs."

1 Timothy 6:10

May

29 What would you learn if you moved to a neighborhood comprised of people from a different culture?

20__ _____

_____

_____

_____

20__ _____

_____

_____

_____

20__ _____

_____

_____

_____

"For there is no difference between Jew and Gentile—the same Lord is Lord of all and richly blesses all who call on him."

Romans 10:12

May  30

What will computers be able to do in 50 years?

20__ _____
_____
_____
_____

20__ _____
_____
_____
_____

20__ _____
_____
_____
_____

"Through him all things were made; without
him nothing was made that has been made."

John 1:3

May  31

What will you name
your next pet?

20__ _____

_____

_____

_____

20__ _____

_____

_____

_____

20__ _____

_____

_____

_____

"The LORD is good to all; he has
compassion on all he has made."

Psalm 145:9

June

1

Why don't people eat what is best for them?

20__ _____
_____
_____
_____

20__ _____
_____
_____
_____

20__ _____
_____
_____
_____

"Do not join those who drink too much wine or gorge themselves on meat."

Proverbs 23:20

June Why don't people exercise?

20__ _____

_____

_____

_____

20__ _____

_____

_____

_____

20__ _____

_____

_____

_____

"Dear friend, I pray that you may
enjoy good health and that all
may go well with you, even as
your soul is getting along well."

3 John 1:2

June

3

Why would people rather send a message than have a conversation?

20__ _____

_____

_____

_____

20__ _____

_____

_____

_____

20__ _____

_____

_____

_____

_____

"Dear children, let us not love with words or speech but with actions and in truth."

1 John 3:18

June

4

What is one way you can show respect to your older sister or mother this week?

20__ _____

_____

_____

_____

20__ _____

_____

_____

_____

20__ _____

_____

_____

_____

"Treat ... older women as mothers, and younger women as sisters, with absolute purity."

1 Timothy 5:1-2

June 5

How can you show respect to your brother or sister this week?

20__ _____

_____

_____

_____

20__ _____

_____

_____

_____

20__ _____

_____

_____

_____

"Treat younger men as brothers."

1 Timothy 5:1

June

Do words hurt more
than sticks and stones?

20__ _____

_____

_____

_____

20__ _____

_____

_____

_____

20__ _____

_____

_____

_____

"The soothing tongue is a tree of life, but
a perverse tongue crushes the spirit."

Proverbs 15:4

June

7

What would it be like if you never brushed your hair?

20__ _____

_____

_____

_____

20__ _____

_____

_____

_____

20__ _____

_____

_____

_____

"Wash and make yourselves clean."

Isaiah 1:16

June

Why does it hurt people when we are selfish?

20__ _____

_____

_____

_____

20__ _____

_____

_____

_____

20__ _____

_____

_____

_____

"He must become greater;
I must become less."

John 3:30

June 9

Why is thinking the best about a person not always our first thought?

20__ _____

_____

_____

_____

20__ _____

_____

_____

_____

20__ _____

_____

_____

_____

"Value others above yourselves."

Philippians 2:3

June

What would the world look like if, for one day, everyone put someone else's needs first?

20__ _____

_____

_____

_____

20__ _____

_____

_____

_____

20__ _____

_____

_____

_____

"No one should seek their own good, but the good of others."

1 Corinthians 10:24

June 11

What puts you in a bad mood?

20__ _____

_____

_____

_____

20__ _____

_____

_____

_____

20__ _____

_____

_____

_____

"Above all else, guard your heart,
for everything you do flows from it."

Proverbs 4:23

June ∘°⟨**12**⟩

What puts you in a good mood?

20__ _____

_____

_____

_____

20__ _____

_____

_____

_____

20__ _____

_____

_____

_____

"Rejoice always."

1 Thessalonians 5:16

June 13

Should your parents adopt a child?

20__ _____

_____

_____

_____

20__ _____

_____

_____

_____

20__ _____

_____

_____

_____

"So in Christ Jesus you are all children of God through faith."

Galatians 3:26

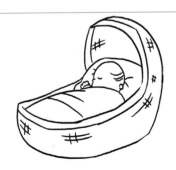

June 14

Why do some people have far more than they need and others have nothig?

20__ _____

_____

_____

_____

20__ _____

_____

_____

_____

20__ _____

_____

_____

_____

"I know what it is to be in need, and I know what it is to have plenty. I have learned the secret of being content in any and every situation."

Philippians 4:12

June  15

Why do flowers make
you feel good?

20__ _____
_____
_____
_____

20__ _____
_____
_____
_____

20__ _____
_____
_____
_____

"The grass withers and the flowers fall,
but the word of our God endures forever."

Isaiah 40:8

June 16

What would it be like to be in the royal family?

20__ _____
_____
_____
_____

20__ _____
_____
_____
_____

20__ _____
_____
_____
_____

"But you are a chosen people, a royal priesthood, a holy nation, God's special possession, that you may declare the praises of him who called you out of darkness into his wonderful light."

1 Peter 2:9

June

17

Why can boys have hair on their legs and girls have to shave?

20__ _____

_____

_____

_____

20__ _____

_____

_____

_____

20__ _____

_____

_____

_____

"Your beauty should not come from outward adornment, such as elaborate hairstyles and the wearing of gold jewelry or fine clothes. Rather, it should be that of your inner self, the unfading beauty of a gentle and quiet spirit, which is of great worth in God's sight."

1 Peter 3:3-4

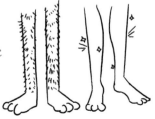

June  18

What makes you laugh the most?

20__ _____
_____
_____
_____

20__ _____
_____
_____
_____

20__ _____
_____
_____
_____

"Therefore my heart is glad,
and my tongue rejoices."

Psalm 16:9

June 19

Will there ever be world peace?

20__ _____

_____

_____

_____

20__ _____

_____

_____

_____

20__ _____

_____

_____

_____

"If it is possible, as far as it depends on you, live at peace with everyone."

Romans 12:18

June  20

What would it be like to be another ethnicity?

20__ _____

_____

_____

_____

20__ _____

_____

_____

_____

20__ _____

_____

_____

_____

"There is neither Jew nor Gentile, neither slave nor free, nor is there male and female, for you are all one in Christ Jesus."

Galatians 3:28

June

What is the difference between a mistake and a bad choice?

20__ _____

_____

_____

_____

20__ _____

_____

_____

_____

20__ _____

_____

_____

_____

"Come now, let us reason together," says the LORD. "Though your sins are like scarlet, they shall be as white as snow; though they are red as crimson, they shall be like wool."

Isaiah 1:18

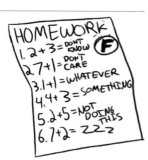

June 22

What would it be like if all your siblings spoke different languages?

20__ _____
_____
_____
_____

20__ _____
_____
_____
_____

20__ _____
_____
_____
_____

"All of them were filled with the Holy Spirit and began to speak in other tongues as the Spirit enabled them."

Acts 2:4

June

23

What would you do if gravity stopped working?

20__ _____

_____

_____

_____

20__ _____

_____

_____

_____

20__ _____

_____

_____

_____

"The Lord makes firm the steps of the one who delights in him; though he may stumble, he will not fall, for the Lord upholds him with his hand."

Psalm 37:23-24

June 24

What changes would you make in your life if you knew you could not die?

20__ _____

_____

_____

_____

20__ _____

_____

_____

_____

20__ _____

_____

_____

_____

"I, wisdom, dwell together with prudence; I possess knowledge and discretion."

Proverbs 8:12

June 25

Do your actions make a difference as to where you will be after you die?

20__ _____

_____

_____

_____

20__ _____

_____

_____

_____

20__ _____

_____

_____

_____

"Whoever sows to please their flesh, from the flesh will reap destruction; whoever sows to please the Spirit, from the Spirit will reap eternal life."

Galatians 6:8

June

26

If you could put up a billboard, what would it say and where would it be?

20__ _____

_____

_____

_____

20__ _____

_____

_____

_____

20__ _____

_____

_____

_____

"He has made everything beautiful in its time. He has also set eternity in the human heart."

Ecclesiastes 3:11

June

27

If you could go back in time 5 years, what advice would you give yourself?

20__ _____

_____

_____

_____

20__ _____

_____

_____

_____

20__ _____

_____

_____

"If any of you lacks wisdom, you should ask God, who gives generously to all without finding fault, and it will be given to you."

James 1:5

June

28 Who is the most successful person you know and why?

20__ _____

_____

_____

_____

20__ _____

_____

_____

_____

20__ _____

_____

_____

_____

"Keep this Book of the Law always on your lips; meditate on it day and night, so that you may be careful to do everything written in it. Then you will be prosperous and successful."

Joshua 1:8

June

29

What is a bad habit you would like to overcome?

20__ _____
_____
_____
_____

20__ _____
_____
_____
_____

20__ _____
_____
_____
_____

"Follow God's example, therefore,
as dearly loved children."

Ephesians 5:1

June  30

What is one word
or phrase that
you use too often?

20__ _____
_____
_____
_____

20__ _____
_____
_____
_____

20__ _____
_____
_____
_____

"The words of the reckless pierce like swords,
but the tongue of the wise brings healing."

Proverbs 12:18

July

1

What is the one thing that influences your life, but you wish it didn't?

20__ _____

_____

_____

_____

20__ _____

_____

_____

_____

20__ _____

_____

_____

_____

"Blessed are those who do not walk in step with the wicked or stand in the way that sinners take or sit in the company of mockers."

Psalm 1:1

July  2

How would you describe the perfect morning routine?

20__ _____

_____

_____

_____

20__ _____

_____

_____

_____

20__ _____

_____

_____

_____

"He wakens me morning by morning, wakens my ear to listen like one being taught."

Isaiah 50:4

July  3

What is one thing you wish you had pursued but didn't?

20__ _____

_____

_____

_____

20__ _____

_____

_____

_____

20__ _____

_____

_____

_____

"Now may the God of peace...equip you with everything good for doing his will, and may he work in us what is pleasing to him."

Hebrews 13:20-21

July  4

What are two ways you can be more creative?

20__ _____

_____

_____

_____

20__ _____

_____

_____

_____

20__ _____

_____

_____

_____

"He has filled him with the Spirit of God, with wisdom, with understanding, with knowledge and with all kinds of skills—to make artistic designs for work in gold, silver and bronze."

Exodus 35:31-32

July

What is the earliest memory you have?

20__ _____

_____

_____

_____

20__ _____

_____

_____

_____

20__ _____

_____

_____

_____

"But Timothy has just now come to us from you and has brought good news about your faith and love. He has told us that you always have pleasant memories of us and that you long to see us, just as we also long to see you."

1 Thessalonians 3:6

July  6

What is your favorite game to play?

20__ _____
_____
_____
_____

20__ _____
_____
_____

20__ _____
_____
_____

"The city streets will
be filled with boys and
girls playing there."

Zechariah 8:5

July

What is your favorite hour of the day?

20__ _____

_____

_____

_____

20__ _____

_____

_____

_____

20__ _____

_____

_____

_____

"God called the light "day," and the darkness
he called "night." And there was evening,
and there was morning - the first day."

Genesis 1:5

July

8

If you could transport yourself anywhere in the world for one hour, where would it be?

20__ _____

_____

_____

_____

20__ _____

_____

_____

_____

20__ _____

_____

_____

_____

"When I consider your heavens, the work of your fingers, the moon and the stars, which you have set in place..."

Psalm 8:3

July

What is the best dream you've ever had?

20__ _____

_____

_____

_____

20__ _____

_____

_____

_____

20__ _____

_____

_____

_____

"The Lord appeared to Solomon during the night in a dream, and God said, "Ask for whatever you want me to give you."

1 Kings 3:5

July  10

What song do you
secretly love?

20__ _____

_____

_____

_____

20__ _____

_____

_____

_____

20__ _____

_____

_____

_____

"Sing and make music from
your heart to the Lord."

Ephesians 5:19

July

What animal makes
the coolest noise?

20__ _____

_____

_____

_____

20__ _____

_____

_____

_____

20__ _____

_____

_____

_____

"The righteous care for the
needs of their animals."

Proverbs 12:10

July

12

What is the worst smell in the world?

20__ _____

_____

_____

_____

20__ _____

_____

_____

_____

20__ _____

_____

_____

_____

"As dead flies give perfume a bad smell, so a little folly outweighs wisdom and honor."

Ecclesiastes 10:1

July  13

What is the best
smell in the world?

20__ _____
_____
_____
_____

20__ _____
_____
_____
_____

20__ _____
_____
_____
_____

"For we are to God the pleasing aroma
of Christ among those who are being
saved and those who are perishing."

2 Corinthians 2:15

July

14

If you could only keep one item from your room, what would it be?

20__ _____

_____

_____

_____

20__ _____

_____

_____

_____

20__ _____

_____

_____

_____

"The gift of God is eternal life in Christ Jesus our Lord."

Romans 6:23

July  15

What is the longest walk you have ever taken?

20__ _____

_____

_____

_____

20__ _____

_____

_____

_____

20__ _____

_____

_____

_____

"When Jesus spoke again to the people, he said, "I am the light of the world. Whoever follows me will never walk in darkness, but will have the light of life."

John 8:12

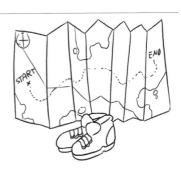

July 16

Who would you trust with your deepest secret?

20__ _____

20__ _____

20__ _____

"When I am afraid, I put my trust in you."

Psalm 56:3

July 17

Who do you know that is terrible at keeping secrets?

20__ _____

_____

_____

_____

20__ _____

_____

_____

_____

20__ _____

_____

_____

_____

"Trust in the LORD forever,
for the LORD, the LORD, is
the Rock eternal."

Isaiah 26:4

July

18

How much would you pay for water if you were stranded in the desert?

20__ _____

_____

_____

_____

20__ _____

_____

_____

_____

20__ _____

_____

_____

_____

"When a Samaritan woman came to draw water, Jesus said to her, "Will you give me a drink?"

John 4:7

July  19

What would you do
if you got lost
from your family?

20__ _____

_____

_____

_____

20__ _____

_____

_____

_____

20__ _____

_____

_____

_____

"May the Lord keep watch
between you and me when we
are away from each other."

Genesis 31:49

July

20

Which do you prefer...
1,000 social media
friends or one true friend?

20__ _____

_____

_____

_____

20__ _____

_____

_____

_____

20__ _____

_____

_____

_____

"A man of too many friends comes
to ruin, but there is a friend who
sticks closer than a brother."

Proverbs 18:24

July 21

What qualities are in a true friend?

20__ _____

_____

_____

_____

20__ _____

_____

_____

_____

20__ _____

_____

_____

_____

"The pleasantness of a friend springs from their heartfelt advice."

Proverbs 27:6

July

22

What should the speed limit be on the highway?

20__ _____

_____

_____

_____

20__ _____

_____

_____

_____

20__ _____

_____

_____

_____

"Remind the people to be subject to rulers and authorities, to be obedient, to be ready to do whatever is good."

Titus 3:1

July  23

Describe the day when we have flying cars?

20__ _____

_____

_____

_____

20__ _____

_____

_____

_____

20__ _____

_____

_____

_____

"Then I saw another angel flying in midair, and he had the eternal gospel to proclaim to those who live on the earth - to every nation, tribe, language and people."

Revelation 14:6

July

24

How would you feel if you encouraged every person you encountered today?

20__ _____

_____

_____

_____

20__ _____

_____

_____

_____

20__ _____

_____

_____

_____

"But encourage one another daily, as long as it is called "Today".

Hebrews 3:13

July How would you feel if everyone you encountered today encouraged you?

20__ _____

_____

_____

_____

20__ _____

_____

_____

_____

20__ _____

_____

_____

_____

"Therefore encourage one another with these words."

1 Thessalonians 4:18

July 26

What is love?

20__ _____

_____

_____

_____

20__ _____

_____

_____

_____

20__ _____

_____

_____

_____

"Love is patient, love is kind. It does not envy, it does not boast, it is not proud."

1 Corinthians 13:4

July  27

Why do you like
receiving gifts?

20__ _____

_____

_____

_____

20__ _____

_____

_____

_____

20__ _____

_____

_____

_____

"Thanks be to God for his
indescribable gift!"

2 Corinthians 9:15

July  28

Is underwear
really necessary?

20__ _____
_____
_____
_____

20__ _____
_____
_____
_____

20__ _____
_____
_____
_____

"Make linen undergarments as a
covering for the body, reaching
from the waist to the thigh."

Exodus 28:42

July What is preventing you from inventing something?

20__ _____

_____

_____

_____

20__ _____

_____

_____

_____

20__ _____

_____

_____

_____

"Know that the LORD is God. It is he who made us, and we are his; we are his people, the sheep of his pasture."

Psalm 100:3

July  30

How do you make
people feel special?

20__ _____
_____
_____
_____
_____

20__ _____
_____
_____
_____
_____

20__ _____
_____
_____
_____
_____

"He cares for you."

1 Peter 5:7

July

How would you complete this statement? I feel special when people...

20__ _____

_____

_____

_____

20__ _____

_____

_____

_____

20__ _____

_____

_____

_____

"Since you are precious and honored in my sight, and because I love you, I will give nations in exchange for you, and peoples in exchange for your life."

Isaiah 43:4

August

1

How many pairs of shoes will you buy in your lifetime?

20__ _____
_____
_____
_____
_____

20__ _____
_____
_____
_____

20__ _____
_____
_____
_____

"How beautiful are the feet of those who bring good news!"

Romans 10:15

August · 2

Would you ever jump out of an airplane?

20__ _____

_____

_____

_____

20__ _____

_____

_____

_____

20__ _____

_____

_____

_____

"Now faith is confidence
in what we hope for and
assurance about what we
do not see."

Hebrews 1:11

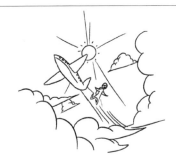

August

3

How would your life be different if you had to walk a mile to fetch water?

20__ _____

_____

_____

_____

20__ _____

_____

_____

_____

20__ _____

_____

_____

_____

"But those who drink the water I give them will never thirst. Indeed, the water I give them will become in them a spring of water welling up to eternal life."

John 4:14

August How many ideas can your brain hold?

20__ _____

_____

_____

_____

20__ _____

_____

_____

_____

20__ _____

_____

_____

_____

"To these four young men God gave
knowledge and understanding of all
kinds of literature and learning. And
Daniel could understand visions and
dreams of all kinds."

Daniel 1:17

August · 5

What is the most disappointed you have ever been?

20__ _____
_____
_____
_____

20__ _____
_____
_____
_____

20__ _____
_____
_____
_____

"The thief comes only to steal and kill and destroy; I have come that they may have life, and have it to the full."

John 10:10

August 6

If you could change your given name, what would you change it to?

20__ _____
_____
_____
_____

20__ _____
_____
_____
_____

20__ _____
_____
_____
_____

"Do not fear, for I have redeemed you; I have summoned you by name; you are mine."

Isaiah 43:1

HELLO, MY NAME IS:
Lord Tigerzilla the III

August

7

What is one way people know you are happy?

20__ _____

_____

_____

_____

20__ _____

_____

_____

_____

20__ _____

_____

_____

_____

"The LORD is my strength and my shield; my heart trusts in him, and he helps me. My heart leaps for joy, and with my song I praise him."

Psalm 28:7

August

What is one way
people know
you are sad?

20__ _____

_____

_____

_____

20__ _____

_____

_____

_____

20__ _____

_____

_____

_____

"Record my misery; list my tears on your
scroll - are they not in your record?"

Psalm 56:8

August

9

What is one thing you would never sell, no matter the price?

20__ _____

_____

_____

_____

20__ _____

_____

_____

_____

20__ _____

_____

_____

_____

"Do you not know that your bodies are temples of the Holy Spirit, who is in you, whom you have received from God? You are not your own; you were bought at a price. Therefore honor God with your bodies."

1 Corinthians 6:19-20

August 10

Which would you rather be...a scientist or an artist? Why?

20__ _____

_____

_____

_____

20__ _____

_____

_____

_____

20__ _____

_____

_____

_____

"So Christ himself gave the apostles, the prophets, the evangelists, the pastors and teachers, to equip his people for works of service."

Ephesians 4:11-12

August

11

How many TVs would you like to have in your house?

20__ _____

_____

_____

_____

20__ _____

_____

_____

_____

20__ _____

_____

_____

_____

"Then he said to them, "Watch out! Be on your guard against all kinds of greed; life does not consist in an abundance of possessions."

Luke 12:15

August  12

What is one movie you are scared to watch?

20__ _____

_____

_____

_____

20__ _____

_____

_____

_____

20__ _____

_____

_____

_____

"I will not set before my eyes anything that is worthless."

Psalm 101:3 (ESV)

August  13

Tell about a time when someone made fun of you.

20__ _____

_____

_____

_____

20__ _____

_____

_____

_____

20__ _____

_____

_____

_____

"So in everything, do to others what you would have them do to you."

Matthew 7:12

August 14

What makes you so mad you would want to hit someone?

20__ _____
_____
_____
_____

20__ _____
_____
_____
_____

20__ _____
_____
_____
_____

"The LORD examines the righteous, but the wicked, those who love violence, he hates with a passion."

Psalm 11:5

August  15

What could bring you to hit your sibling?

20__ _____

_____

_____

_____

20__ _____

_____

_____

_____

20__ _____

_____

_____

_____

" I hate it when people clothe themselves with injustice," says the LORD Almighty. So be on your guard, and do not be unfaithful."

Malachi 2:16

August 16

Who makes you laugh when you see his or her face?

20__ _____
_____
_____
_____

20__ _____
_____
_____
_____

20__ _____
_____
_____
_____

"Whoever mocks the poor shows contempt for their Maker."

Proverbs 17:5

August 17

How do other people describe you to their friends?

20__ _____

_____

_____

_____

20__ _____

_____

_____

_____

20__ _____

_____

_____

_____

"A faithful person who can find?"

Proverbs 20:6

August  18

Would you rather go for a bike ride or play a video game?

20__ _____

_____

_____

_____

20__ _____

_____

_____

_____

20__ _____

_____

_____

_____

"Anyone who chooses to be a friend of the world becomes an enemy of God."

James 4:4

August · 19

Would you rather go to a party or have one friend over?

20__ _____
_____
_____
_____

20__ _____
_____
_____
_____

20__ _____
_____
_____
_____

"Above all, love each other deeply, because love covers over a multitude of sins. Offer hospitality to one another without grumbling."

1 Peter 4:8-9

August  20

Would you keep a friend's secret if you knew he or she needed help?

20__ _____
_____
_____
_____

20__ _____
_____
_____

20__ _____
_____
_____

"If any one of you has material possessions and sees a brother or sister in need but has no pity on them, how can the love of God be in you?"

1 John 3:17

August

21

What unique gift do you possess?

20__ _____

_____

_____

_____

20__ _____

_____

_____

_____

20__ _____

_____

_____

_____

"We have different gifts, according to the grace given to each of us."

Romans 12:6

August 22

If you could start a new family tradition, what would it be?

20__ _____
_____
_____
_____

20__ _____
_____
_____
_____

20__ _____
_____
_____
_____

"When he was twelve years old, they went up to the festival, according to the custom."

Luke 2:42

August

23

What character in a book or movie would you like to have as your best friend?

20__ _____

_____

_____

_____

20__ _____

_____

_____

_____

20__ _____

_____

_____

_____

"I have called you friends, for everything that I learned from my Father I have made known to you."

John 15:15

August  24

What three words would you use to describe your mother?

20__ _____

_____

_____

_____

20__ _____

_____

_____

_____

20__ _____

_____

_____

_____

"She is clothed with strength and dignity;
she can laugh at the days to come."

Proverbs 31:25

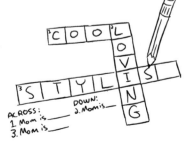

ACROSS:
1. Mom is____
3. Mom is____

DOWN:
2. Mom is____

August 25

What three words would you use to describe your father?

20__ _____
_____
_____
_____

20__ _____
_____
_____
_____

20__ _____
_____
_____
_____

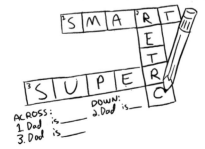

ACROSS:
1. Dad is ____
3. Dad is ____

DOWN:
2. Dad is ____

"The righteous lead blameless lives; blessed are their children after them."

Proverbs 20:7

August  26

How would you describe the perfect school?

20__ _____

_____

_____

_____

20__ _____

_____

_____

_____

20__ _____

_____

_____

_____

"You gave your good
Spirit to instruct them."

Nehemiah 9:20

August  27

How would you describe the perfect teacher?

20__ _____
_____
_____
_____
_____

20__ _____
_____
_____
_____

20__ _____
_____
_____
_____

"In your teaching show integrity, seriousness and soundness of speech."

Titus 2:7-8

August  28

If you had all the
time in the world,
what would you do?

20__ _____

_____

_____

_____

20__ _____

_____

_____

_____

20__ _____

_____

_____

_____

"Making the best use of
the time, because the
days are evil."

Ephesians 5:16 (ESV)

August ..°29

How much money do you want to have before you retire?

20__ _____

_____

_____

_____

20__ _____

_____

_____

_____

20__ _____

_____

_____

_____

"No one can serve two masters. Either you will hate the one and love the other, or you will be devoted to the one and despise the other. You cannot serve both God and money."

Matthew 6:24

August  30

What is your
proudest moment?

20__ _____

_____

_____

_____

20__ _____

_____

_____

_____

20__ _____

_____

_____

_____

"We are not trying to commend ourselves to
you again, but are giving you an opportunity
to take pride in us, so that you can answer
those who take pride in what is seen rather
than in what is in the heart."

2 Corinthians 5:12

August  31

How do you know what is right or wrong?

20__ _____

_____

_____

_____

20__ _____

_____

_____

_____

20__ _____

_____

_____

_____

"Reflect on what I am saying, for the Lord will give you insight into all this."

2 Timothy 2:7

September

1

What is one challenge your grandchildren will face?

20__ _____

_____

_____

_____

20__ _____

_____

_____

_____

20__ _____

_____

_____

_____

"No temptation has overtaken you except what is common to us all. And God is faithful; he will not let you be tempted beyond what you can bear. But when you are tempted, he will also provide a way out so that you can endure it."

1 Corinthians 10:13

September

2

If you could smell one thing first thing in the morning, what would it be?

20__ _____

_____

_____

_____

20__ _____

_____

_____

_____

20__ _____

_____

_____

_____

"Pleasing is the fragrance of your perfumes; your name is like perfume poured out."

Song of Solomon 1:3

September

Have you ever lied to a friend?

20__ _____

_____

_____

_____

20__ _____

_____

_____

_____

20__ _____

_____

_____

_____

"Keep your tongue from evil."

Psalm 34:13

September

20__ _____

_____

_____

_____

20__ _____

_____

_____

_____

20__ _____

_____

_____

_____

"Those who have been stealing must steal no longer, but must work, doing something useful with their own hands, that they may have something to share with those in need."

Ephesians 4:28

September

What are two adjectives you'd like people to use when describing you?

20__ _____

_____

_____

_____

20__ _____

_____

_____

_____

20__ _____

_____

_____

_____

"Make every effort to add to your faith goodness; and to goodness, knowledge; and to knowledge, self-control; and to self-control, perseverance; and to perseverance, godliness; and to godliness, mutual affection; and to mutual affection, love."

2 Peter 1:5-7

September 6

Where will you celebrate your birthday in five years?

20__ _____

_____

_____

_____

20__ _____

_____

_____

_____

20__ _____

_____

_____

_____

"You cannot discover any-
thing about your future."

Ecclesiastes 7:14

September

7 What would it be like if you didn't have a family to come home to?

20__ _____

_____

_____

_____

20__ _____

_____

_____

_____

20__ _____

_____

_____

_____

"Religion that God our Father accepts as pure and faultless is this: to look after orphans and widows."

James 1:27

September How many other galaxies are there in the universe?

20__ _____

_____

_____

_____

20__ _____

_____

_____

_____

20__ _____

_____

_____

_____

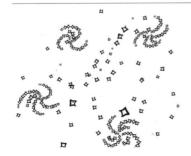

"He determines the number of the stars and calls them each by name."

Psalms 147:4

September

9

Who will be a part
of your most
favorite memory?

20__ _____

_____

_____

_____

20__ _____

_____

_____

_____

20__ _____

_____

_____

_____

"Jesus, remember me
when you come into your
kingdom."

Luke 23:42

September What happens if you break a rule at home?

20__ _____

_____

_____

_____

20__ _____

_____

_____

_____

20__ _____

_____

_____

_____

Then Jesus came to them and said, "All authority in heaven and on earth has been given to me."

Matthew 28:18

September

11 Why do we often treat people who are different from us differently?

20__ _____

_____

_____

_____

20__ _____

_____

_____

_____

20__ _____

_____

_____

_____

"Who is like the Lord our God, the One who sits enthroned on high, who stoops down to look on the heavens and the earth? He raises the poor from the dust and lifts the needy from the ash heap; he seats them with princes, with the princes of his people."

Psalm 113:5-8

September

12 What will your face look like when you are 80?

20__ _____

_____

_____

_____

20__ _____

_____

_____

_____

20__ _____

_____

_____

_____

"Gray hair is a crown of splendor; it is attained in the way of righteousness."

Proverbs 16:31

September 13

Who do you think you will love the most in your life?

20__ _____

_____

_____

_____

20__ _____

_____

_____

_____

20__ _____

_____

_____

_____

"'Love your neighbor as yourself.' There is no commandment greater than these."

Mark 12:31

September

14 What can you do about people in your community who may not eat a meal today?

20__ _____

_____

_____

_____

20__ _____

_____

_____

_____

20__ _____

_____

_____

_____

"Those who give to the poor will lack nothing."

Proverbs 28:27

September

If you were without electricity, what are the steps you would take to prepare a meal?

20__ _____

_____

_____

_____

20__ _____

_____

_____

_____

20__ _____

_____

_____

_____

"When they landed, they saw a fire of burning coals there with fish on it, and some bread. Jesus said to them, "Bring some of the fish you have just caught."

John 21:9-10

September

What is the first thing you would do if you won the lottery?

20__ _____

_____

_____

_____

20__ _____

_____

_____

_____

20__ _____

_____

_____

_____

"Do not withhold good from those to whom it is due, when it is in your power to act. Do not say to your neighbor, "Come back tomorrow and I'll give it to you"—when you already have it with you."

Proverbs 3:27-28

September

17

How big will your ears will be when you are 80? What about your nose?

20__ _____

_____

_____

_____

20__ _____

_____

_____

_____

20__ _____

_____

_____

_____

"Is not wisdom found among the aged?
Does not long life bring understanding?"

Job 12:12

September 18

How many miles do you think you can run?

20__ _____

_____

_____

_____

20__ _____

_____

_____

_____

20__ _____

_____

_____

_____

0.1 MILE

"Let us run with perse-
verance the race marked
out for us."

Hebrews 12:1

September · 19

Do you prefer team sports or individual sports?

20__ _____

_____

_____

_____

20__ _____

_____

_____

_____

20__ _____

_____

_____

_____

"from him the whole body, joined and held together by every supporting ligament, grows and builds itself up in love, as each part does its work."

Ephesians 4:16

September

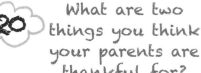

What are two things you think your parents are thankful for?

20__ _____

_____

_____

_____

20__ _____

_____

_____

_____

20__ _____

_____

_____

_____

"Children, obey your parents in everything, for this pleases the Lord."

Colossians 3:20

September

What are two things you love about the person to your right?

20__ _____

_____

_____

_____

20__ _____

_____

_____

_____

20__ _____

_____

_____

_____

"Whatever is true, whatever is noble, whatever is right, whatever is pure, whatever is lovely, whatever is admirable—if anything is excellent or praiseworthy—think about such things."

Philippians 4:8

September

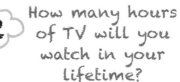

22

How many hours of TV will you watch in your lifetime?

20__ _____

_____

_____

_____

20__ _____

_____

_____

_____

20__ _____

_____

_____

_____

"The eye is the lamp of the body. If your eyes are healthy, your whole body will be full of light."

Matthew 6:22

September

23

When you meet someone new, do you assume the best or the worst about that person?

20__ _____

_____

_____

_____

20__ _____

_____

_____

_____

20__ _____

_____

_____

_____

"Do not judge, or you too will be judged."

Matthew 7:1

September 24

What is the best thing you can put in your body?

20__ _____

_____

_____

_____

20__ _____

_____

_____

_____

20__ _____

_____

_____

_____

"Therefore, I urge you, brothers and sisters, in view of God's mercy, to offer your bodies as a living sacrifice, holy and pleasing to God—this is your true and proper worship."

Romans 12:1

September 25

What is the worst thing you can put in your body?

20__ _____

_____

_____

_____

20__ _____

_____

_____

_____

20__ _____

_____

_____

_____

"Don't you know that you yourselves are God's temple and that God's Spirit dwells in your midst? If anyone destroys God's temple, God will destroy that person; for God's temple is sacred, and you together are that temple."

1 Corinthians 3:16-17

September

26

Would you rather spend a week in the mountains or at the beach?

20__ _____

_____

_____

_____

20__ _____

_____

_____

_____

20__ _____

_____

_____

_____

"Come to me, all you who are weary and burdened, and I will give you rest."

Matthew 11:28

September **27**

What is the best meal your mom makes?

20__ _____

_____

_____

_____

20__ _____

_____

_____

_____

20__ _____

_____

_____

_____

So Abraham hurried into the tent to Sarah. "Quick," he said, "get three seahs of the finest flour and knead it and bake some bread."

Genesis 18:6

September **28**

What is the
best meal your
dad makes?

20__ _____

_____

_____

_____

20__ _____

_____

_____

_____

20__ _____

_____

_____

_____

"For he satisfies the thirsty
and fills the hungry with
good things."

Psalms 107:9

September

29 What is more important to you ... winning a game or making friends?

20__ _____

_____

_____

_____

20__ _____

_____

_____

_____

20__ _____

_____

_____

_____

"Each of you should test your own actions. Then you can take pride in yourself, without comparing yourself to somebody else."

Galatians 6:4

September

Would you rather take a math test or write a paper?

30

20__ _____

_____

_____

_____

20__ _____

_____

_____

_____

20__ _____

_____

_____

_____

BOOK REPORT

2 + 2 =
4 + 6 =
7 + 4 =
8 + 1 =

"To these four young men God gave knowledge and understanding of all kinds of literature and learning."

Daniel 1:17

October 1

Which is more important to you, having a big house or a big yard?

20__ _____

_____

_____

_____

20__ _____

_____

_____

_____

20__ _____

_____

_____

_____

"By wisdom a house is built, and through understanding it is established; through knowledge its rooms are filled with rare and beautiful treasures."

Proverbs 24:3-4

October · 2

What is the most creative thing you have done this week?

20__ _____
_____
_____
_____

20__ _____
_____
_____
_____

20__ _____
_____
_____
_____

"How many are your works, LORD! In wisdom you made them all; the earth is full of your creatures."

Psalms 104:24

October · 3

What can you learn from your grandparents?

20__ _____

_____

_____

_____

20__ _____

_____

_____

_____

20__ _____

_____

_____

_____

"Remember your leaders, who spoke the word of God to you. Consider the outcome of their way of life and imitate their faith."

Hebrews 13:7

October

4 What are some ways to thank a service member?

20__ _____

_____

_____

_____

20__ _____

_____

_____

_____

20__ _____

_____

_____

_____

"May the LORD repay you for what you have done."

Ruth 2:12

October Would you rather be on stage or back-stage?

20__ _____

_____

_____

_____

20__ _____

_____

_____

_____

20__ _____

_____

_____

_____

"The night is nearly over; the day is almost here. So let us put aside the deeds of darkness and put on the armor of light."

Romans 13:12

October 6

When you meet a new person, are you more likely to ask a question or answer a question?

20__ _____

_____

_____

_____

20__ _____

_____

_____

_____

20__ _____

_____

_____

_____

"When they came to Jerusalem, they were welcomed by the church and the apostles and elders, to whom they reported everything God had done through them."

Acts 15:4

October 7

How do you react when you accomplish a goal?

20__ _____

_____

_____

_____

20__ _____

_____

_____

_____

20__ _____

_____

_____

_____

"May he give you the desire of your heart and make all your plans succeed."

Psalm 20:4

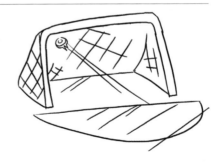

October · · 8

How do you react
when you fail to
reach a goal?

20__ _____

_____

_____

_____

20__ _____

_____

_____

_____

20__ _____

_____

_____

_____

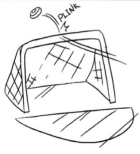

"When people fall down,
do they not get up?"

Jeremiah 8:4

October 9

Do you like a routine schedule or do you prefer to go with the flow?

20__ _____

_____

_____

_____

20__ _____

_____

_____

_____

20__ _____

_____

_____

_____

"Do your best to present yourself to God as one approved, a worker who does not need to be ashamed and who correctly handles the word of truth."

2 Timothy 2:15

October 10

How many toys
are currently
under your bed?

20__ _____

_____

_____

_____

20__ _____

_____

_____

_____

20__ _____

_____

_____

_____

KEEP OUT!
SECRET FORT

"Set your minds on things
above, not on earthly things."

Colossians 3:2

October · 11

If you had $100, how many dollars would you give away?

20__ _____

_____

_____

_____

20__ _____

_____

_____

_____

20__ _____

_____

_____

_____

"The generous will themselves be blessed, for they share their food with the poor."

Proverbs 22:9

October

12

If you could give $100 to anyone or any organization, who would it be?

20__ _____

_____

_____

_____

20__ _____

_____

_____

_____

20__ _____

_____

_____

_____

"Whoever refreshes others will be refreshed."

Proverbs 11:25

October · · ° 13

What activity takes
the most courage?

20__ _____

_____

_____

_____

20__ _____

_____

_____

_____

20__ _____

_____

_____

_____

"Be strong and courageous. Do not be afraid;
do not be discouraged, for the Lord your
God will be with you wherever you go."

Joshua 1:9

October 14

Would you rather sit on the front row or the back row of the classroom?

20__ _____

_____

_____

_____

20__ _____

_____

_____

_____

20__ _____

_____

_____

_____

"Now go; I will help you speak and will teach you what to say."

Exodus 4:12

October · 15

Do most of your friends do the right things or the wrong things?

20__ _____

_____

_____

_____

20__ _____

_____

_____

_____

20__ _____

_____

_____

_____

" If anyone, then, knows the good they ought to do and doesn't do it, it is sin for them."

James 4:17

October 16

What is your favorite cartoon?

20__ _____
_____
_____
_____

20__ _____
_____
_____
_____

20__ _____
_____
_____
_____

"Be alert and of sober mind."

1 Peter 5:8

October ∘∘ 17

Would you rather create an idea or solve a problem?

20__ _____

_____

_____

_____

20__ _____

_____

_____

_____

20__ _____

_____

_____

_____

"But the Advocate, the Holy Spirit, whom the Father will send in my name, will teach you all things and will remind you of everything I have said to you."

John 14:26

October 18

If you were to jump from a high dive, would you rather be the first to try it or would you wait for others to go?

20__ _____

_____

_____

_____

20__ _____

_____

_____

_____

20__ _____

_____

_____

_____

"Set an example for the believers in speech, in conduct, in love, in faith and in purity."

1 Timothy 4:12

October · 19

How important is having a clean appearance? Why?

20__ _____

_____

_____

_____

20__ _____

_____

_____

_____

20__ _____

_____

_____

_____

"Wash and make yourselves clean."

Isaiah 1:16

October · 20

What are you going to be for Halloween?

20__ _____

_____

_____

_____

20__ _____

_____

_____

_____

20__ _____

_____

_____

_____

"Dear friend, do not imitate what is evil but what is good. Anyone who does what is good is from God. Anyone who does what is evil has not seen God."

3 John 1:11

October · 21

Do you like to make quick decisions, or do you like to take your time?

20__ _____

_____

_____

_____

20__ _____

_____

_____

_____

20__ _____

_____

_____

_____

"For the LORD gives wisdom; from his mouth come knowledge and understanding."

Proverbs 2:6

October · 22

What color would you paint your room if you were allowed?

20__ _____

_____

_____

_____

20__ _____

_____

_____

_____

20__ _____

_____

_____

_____

"With all my resources I have provided for the temple of my God - gold for the gold work, silver for the silver, bronze for the bronze, iron for the iron and wood for the wood, as well as onyx for the settings, turquoise, stones of various colors, and all kinds of fine stone and marble - all of these in large quantities." 1

Chronicles 29:2

October 23

If you could give everyone on the planet one thing, what would it be?

20__ _____

_____

_____

_____

20__ _____

_____

_____

_____

20__ _____

_____

_____

_____

"But God demonstrates his own love for us in this: While we were still sinners, Christ died for us."

Romans 5:8

October  24

Why does the truth hurt sometimes?

20__ _____

_____

_____

_____

20__ _____

_____

_____

_____

20__ _____

_____

_____

_____

"Speaking the truth in love, we will
in all things grow up into him
who is the head, that is, Christ."

Ephesians 4:15

October 25

At what have you worked hard and accomplished?

20__ _____

_____

_____

_____

20__ _____

_____

_____

_____

20__ _____

_____

_____

"Whatever you do, work
at it with all your heart,
as working for the Lord,
not for men."

Colossians 3:23

October ∘∘ **26**

When are you
most nervous?

20__ _____

_____

_____

_____

20__ _____

_____

_____

_____

20__ _____

_____

_____

_____

"For he will command his angels concerning
you to guard you in all your ways."

Psalm 91:11

October · 27

What would it be like if your parents were movie stars?

20__ _____

_____

_____

_____

20__ _____

_____

_____

_____

20__ _____

_____

_____

_____

"Honor your father and your mother, so that you may live long in the land the LORD your God is giving you."

Exodus 20:12

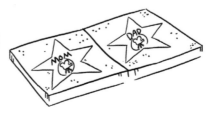

October · · °28

When do you have
the highest level
of anticipation?

20__ _____

_____

_____

_____

20__ _____

_____

_____

_____

20__ _____

_____

_____

_____

"I wait for the LORD, my
whole being waits, and in
his word I put my hope."

Psalms 130:5

October

29

Where is one place you would like to travel this year?

20__ _____

_____

_____

_____

20__ _____

_____

_____

_____

20__ _____

_____

_____

_____

"Go into all the world and preach
the gospel to all creation."

Mark 16:15

October · 30

What people group do you find the most intriguing?

20__ _____

_____

_____

_____

20__ _____

_____

_____

_____

20__ _____

_____

_____

_____

"To the Jews I became like a Jew, to win the Jews. To those under the law I became like one under the law (though I myself am not under the law), so as to win those under the law."

1 Corinthians 9:20

October Should everything in life be fair? Why?

20__ _____

_____

_____

_____

20__ _____

_____

_____

_____

20__ _____

_____

_____

_____

"Masters, provide your slaves
with what is right and fair,
because you know that you
also have a Master in heaven."

Colossians 4:1

November

1 What is your funniest joke?

20__ _____

_____

_____

_____

20__ _____

_____

_____

_____

20__ _____

_____

_____

_____

"Be careful, however, that the exercise of your rights does not become a stumbling block to the weak."

1 Corinthians 8:9

November

2

If you had to eat the same lunch every day, what would it be?

20__ _____

_____

_____

_____

20__ _____

_____

_____

_____

20__ _____

_____

_____

_____

"This is what the LORD has commanded: 'Take an omer of manna and keep it for the generations to come, so they can see the bread I gave you to eat in the wilderness when I brought you out of Egypt."

Exodus 16:32

November

3 What is the most difficult thing about being your age?

20__ _____

_____

_____

_____

20__ _____

_____

_____

_____

20__ _____

_____

_____

_____

YOU MUST BE THIS TALL TO RIDE:

"There is a time for everything, and a season for every activity under the heavens."

Ecclesiastes 3:1

November What would you do if you could control time?

20__ _____

_____

_____

_____

20__ _____

_____

_____

_____

20__ _____

_____

_____

_____

"Let us not become weary in doing good, for at the proper time we will reap a harvest if we do not give up."

Galatians 6:9

November

5 Would you rather have a surprise party or a planned party?

20__ _____

_____

_____

_____

20__ _____

_____

_____

_____

20__ _____

_____

_____

_____

"The LORD has done it this very day; let us rejoice today and be glad."

Psalms 118:24

November · · 6

When have you
been the most
surprised?

20__ _____

_____

_____

_____

20__ _____

_____

_____

_____

20__ _____

_____

_____

_____

"See, I am about to do something
in Israel that will make the ears of
everyone who hears about it tingle."

1 Samuel 3:11

November

7 Would you rather scare someone or be scared?

20__ _____

_____

_____

_____

_____

20__ _____

_____

_____

_____

20__ _____

_____

_____

_____

"But test them all; hold
on to what is good."

1 Thessalonians 5:21

November

20__ _____

_____

_____

_____

20__ _____

_____

_____

_____

20__ _____

_____

_____

_____

8

What emotions do you feel when you see someone being cruel to another person or animal?

"Those who are kind benefit themselves, but the cruel bring ruin on themselves."

Proverbs 11:17

November

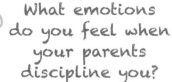

What emotions do you feel when your parents discipline you?

20__ _____

_____

_____

_____

20__ _____

_____

_____

_____

20__ _____

_____

_____

_____

"Children, obey your parents in the Lord, for this is right."

Ephesians 6:1

November · ° 10

What is one thing you are envious of?

20__ _____
_____
_____
_____

20__ _____
_____
_____
_____

20__ _____
_____
_____
_____

"Therefore, rid yourselves of all malice and all deceit, hypocrisy, envy, and slander of every kind."

1 Peter 2:1

November

11

What is one thing you think people envy about you?

20__ _____

_____

_____

_____

20__ _____

_____

_____

_____

20__ _____

_____

_____

_____

"A heart at peace gives life to the body, but envy rots the bones."

Proverbs 14:30

November · 12

Why do you think it feels weird to have no clothes on in public?

20__ _____

_____

_____

_____

20__ _____

_____

_____

_____

20__ _____

_____

_____

_____

"The Lord God made garments of skin for Adam and his wife and clothed them."

Genesis 3:21

November

13 What is one piece of technology you think should be invented?

20__ _____

_____

_____

_____

20__ _____

_____

_____

_____

20__ _____

_____

_____

_____

"for the word of the Lord is right and true."

Psalm 33:4

November 14

What would it be like if you slept with your family on a dirt floor?

20__ _____

_____

_____

_____

20__ _____

_____

_____

_____

20__ _____

_____

_____

_____

"I lie down and sleep; I wake again, because the LORD sustains me."

Psalm 3:5

November  15

Who makes
you feel the
most special?

20__ _____

_____

_____

_____

20__ _____

_____

_____

_____

20__ _____

_____

_____

_____

"For he chose us in him before the creation of the world."

Ephesians 1:4

November Will you ever have a mentor?

20__ _____

_____

_____

_____

20__ _____

_____

_____

_____

20__ _____

_____

_____

_____

"And the things you have heard me say in the presence of many witnesses entrust to reliable people who will also be qualified to teach others."

2 Timothy 2:2

November

°° **17**

Will you ever mentor anyone? If so, who?

20__ _____

20__ _____

20__ _____

"As iron sharpens iron, so one person sharpens another."

Proverbs 27:17

November

18 Is there someone you feel like sending a note to? Do it!

20__ _____

_____

_____

_____

20__ _____

_____

_____

_____

20__ _____

_____

_____

_____

"Dear friends, this is now my second letter to you. I have written both of them as reminders to stimulate you to wholesome thinking."

2 Peter 3:1

November · · 19

If you could send yourself a letter that you would receive in 10 years, what would it say?

20__ _____
_____
_____
_____
_____

20__ _____
_____
_____
_____
_____

20__ _____
_____
_____
_____
_____

"You yourselves are our letter, written on our hearts, known and read by everyone."

2 Corinthians 3:2

November 20

Tell your life story in seven words or less.

20__ _____
_____
_____
_____

20__ _____
_____
_____
_____

20__ _____
_____
_____
_____

"For it is by grace you have been saved, through faith."

Ephesians 2:8

November · 21

What is the greatest adventure you have ever had?

20__ _____
_____
_____
_____

20__ _____
_____
_____
_____

20__ _____
_____
_____
_____

"Come, follow me," Jesus said, "and I will send you out to fish for people."

Matthew 4:19

November ○○ 22

What is your favorite way to celebrate?

20__ _____

_____

_____

_____

20__ _____

_____

_____

_____

20__ _____

_____

_____

_____

"Then all the people went away to eat and drink, to send portions of food and to celebrate with great joy, because they now understood the words that had been made known to them."

Nehemiah 8:12

November 23

How many candy bars will you eat in your lifetime?

20__ _____

_____

_____

_____

20__ _____

_____

_____

_____

20__ _____

_____

_____

_____

"But godliness with contentment is great gain."

1 Timothy 6:6-8

November 24

Have you ever
felt like you
were invisible?
If so, when?

20__ _____

_____

_____

_____

20__ _____

_____

_____

_____

20__ _____

_____

_____

_____

"Be careful not to practice your
righteousness in front of others
to be seen by them."

Matthew 6:1

November 25

Do you ever feel lonely? If so, when?

20__ _____
_____
_____
_____

20__ _____
_____
_____
_____

20__ _____
_____
_____
_____

"Turn to me and be gracious to me, for I am lonely and afflicted."

Psalm 25:16

November 26

What are two ways you might disappoint your parents?

20__ _____

_____

_____

_____

20__ _____

_____

_____

_____

20__ _____

_____

_____

_____

"Do everything without grumbling or arguing."

Philippians 2:14

November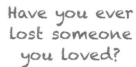

Have you ever lost someone you loved?

20__ _____

_____

_____

_____

20__ _____

_____

_____

_____

20__ _____

_____

_____

_____

"He will wipe every tear from their eyes. There will be no more death' or mourning or crying or pain, for the old order of things has passed away."

Revelation 21:4

November 28

Do you ever have FOMO (Fear Of Missing Out)?

20__ _____

_____

_____

_____

20__ _____

_____

_____

_____

20__ _____

_____

_____

_____

"What is more, I consider
everything a loss because
of the surpassing worth
of knowing Christ Jesus
my Lord, for whose sake
I have lost all things."

Philippians 3:8

November

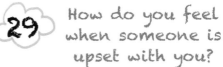

29 How do you feel when someone is upset with you?

20__ _____

_____

_____

_____

20__ _____

_____

_____

_____

20__ _____

_____

_____

_____

"The heart of the righteous weighs its answers."

Proverbs 15:28

November 30

How do you feel when you see someone you love sick?

20__ _____

_____

_____

_____

20__ _____

_____

_____

_____

20__ _____

_____

_____

_____

"The LORD is close to the brokenhearted and saves those who are crushed in spirit."

Psalms 34:18

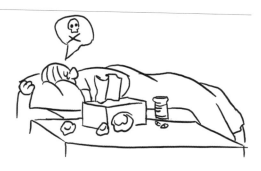

December ○ ○ 💭 1

What's the best way to pass the time on a long road trip?

20__ _____

_____

_____

_____

20__ _____

_____

_____

_____

20__ _____

_____

_____

_____

"Rejoice always, pray continually, give thanks in all circumstances; for this is God's will for you in Christ Jesus."

1 Thessalonians 5:16-18

December · 2

Do outward looks matter?

20__ _____

_____

_____

_____

20__ _____

_____

_____

_____

20__ _____

_____

_____

_____

"But the Lord said to Samuel, "Do not consider
his appearance or his height, for I have rejected
him. The Lord does not look at the things people
look at. People look at the outward appearance,
but the Lord looks at the heart."

1 Samuel 16:7

December

3 How many is too many friends?

20__ _____

_____

_____

_____

20__ _____

_____

_____

_____

20__ _____

_____

_____

_____

"Two are better than one, because they have a good return for their labor: if either of them falls down, one can help the other up."

Ecclesiastes 4:9-10

December · 4

If you could start your own national holiday, what would it be in celebration of?

20__ _____
_____
_____
_____

20__ _____
_____
_____
_____

20__ _____
_____
_____

"As the time when the Jews got relief from their enemies, and as the month when their sorrow was turned into joy and their mourning into a day of celebration. He wrote them to observe the days as days of feasting and joy and giving presents of food to one another and gifts to the poor."

Esther 9:22

December... 5

What is something you've said that you wish you could unsay?

20__ _____

_____

_____

_____

20__ _____

_____

_____

_____

20__ _____

_____

_____

_____

"Let your conversation be always full of grace, seasoned with salt, so that you may know how to answer everyone."

Colossians 4:6

December ⋅ 6

What is something you've seen that you wish you could unsee?

20__ _____

_____

_____

_____

20__ _____

_____

_____

_____

20__ _____

_____

_____

_____

"For God knows that when you eat of it your eyes will be opened, and you will be like God, knowing good and evil."

Genesis 3:5

December 7

What Olympic event would you like to compete in?

20__ _____

_____

_____

_____

20__ _____

_____

_____

_____

20__ _____

_____

_____

_____

"Do you not know that in a race all the runners run, but only one gets the prize?"

1 Corinthians 9:24

December

What is your favorite thing to do in the summer?

20__ _____

_____

_____

_____

20__ _____

_____

_____

_____

20__ _____

_____

_____

_____

"It was you who set all the boundaries of the earth; you made both summer and winter."

Psalms 74:17

December

9

What is your favorite thing to do in the winter?

20__ _____
_____
_____
_____

20__ _____
_____
_____
_____

20__ _____
_____
_____
_____

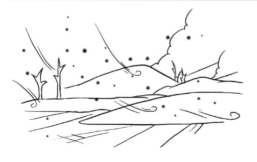

"Perhaps I will stay with you for a while, or even spend the winter, so that you can help me on my journey, wherever I go."

1 Corinthians 16:6

December 10

What is the best thing you have ever constructed?

20__ _____

_____

_____

_____

20__ _____

_____

_____

_____

20__ _____

_____

_____

_____

"Suppose one of you wants to build a tower. Won't you first sit down and estimate the cost to see if you have enough money to complete it?"

Luke 14:28

December

11

Why is it bad for your brain to watch too much tv?

20__ _____

_____

_____

_____

20__ _____

_____

_____

_____

20__ _____

_____

_____

_____

Do not be misled: "Bad company corrupts good character."

1 Corinthians 15:33

December · 12

How would your actions and words change if you were followed around 24/7 by a TV crew?

20__ _____

_____

_____

_____

20__ _____

_____

_____

_____

20__ _____

_____

_____

_____

"Fools find no pleasure in understanding but delight in airing their own opinions."

Proverbs 18:2

December What are two ways you could lose a friend?

20__ _____

_____

_____

_____

20__ _____

_____

_____

_____

20__ _____

_____

_____

_____

"A faithful person who can find?"

Proverbs 20:6

December What are two ways you could gain a friend?

20__ _____

_____

_____

_____

20__ _____

_____

_____

_____

20__ _____

_____

_____

_____

"In everything set them
an example by doing
what is good."

Titus 2:7

December · °° 15

20__ _____

_____

_____

_____

20__ _____

_____

_____

_____

20__ _____

_____

_____

_____

"For God so loved the world that
he gave his one and only Son, that
whoever believes in him shall not
perish but have eternal life."

John 3:16

December · 16

What could you do if you really believed you were unconditionally loved?

20__ _____

_____

_____

_____

20__ _____

_____

_____

_____

20__ _____

_____

_____

_____

"Your love, LORD, reaches to the heavens,
your faithfulness to the skies."

Psalm 36:5

December 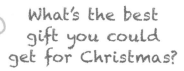 17

What's the best gift you could get for Christmas?

20__ _____

_____

_____

_____

20__ _____

_____

_____

_____

20__ _____

_____

_____

_____

"Every good and perfect gift is from above, coming down from the Father of the heavenly lights."

James 1:17

December

18

What's the best gift you could give for Christmas?

20__ _____

_____

_____

_____

20__ _____

_____

_____

_____

20__ _____

_____

_____

_____

"God loves a cheerful giver."

2 Corinthians 9:7

December · 19

What is your favorite Christmas tradition?

20__ _____

_____

_____

_____

20__ _____

_____

_____

_____

20__ _____

_____

_____

_____

"Glory to God in the highest heaven, and on earth peace to those on whom his favor rests."

Luke 2:14

December · 20

What is your favorite Christmas movie?

20__ _____

_____

_____

_____

20__ _____

_____

_____

_____

20__ _____

_____

_____

_____

"She will give birth to a son, and you are to give him the name Jesus, because he will save his people from their sins."

Matthew 1:21

December

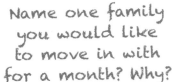

21

Name one family you would like to move in with for a month? Why?

20__ _____

_____

_____

_____

20__ _____

_____

_____

_____

20__ _____

_____

_____

_____

"My people will live in peaceful dwelling places, in secure homes, in undisturbed places of rest."

Isaiah 32:18

December · 22

Name two people who encouraged you this week. What did they do?

20__ _____

_____

_____

_____

20__ _____

_____

_____

_____

20__ _____

_____

_____

_____

"Similarly, encourage the young men to be self-controlled."

Titus 2:6

December 23

Name two people
you encouraged
this week. What
did you do?

20__ _____

_____

_____

_____

20__ _____

_____

_____

_____

20__ _____

_____

_____

_____

"I am sending him to you ...that
he may encourage your hearts."

Colossians 4:8

December 24

If you could play a character in a movie, who would it be?

20__ _____

_____

_____

_____

20__ _____

_____

_____

_____

20__ _____

_____

_____

_____

"Follow my example, as I follow the example of Christ."

1 Corinthians 11:1

December

25

What thing made you the most angry this week? How did you handle it?

20__ _____

_____

_____

_____

20__ _____

_____

_____

_____

20__ _____

_____

_____

_____

"In your anger do not sin."

Ephesians 4:26

December

26 Name a time when you didn't care about what other people thought of you?

20__ _____

_____

_____

_____

20__ _____

_____

_____

_____

20__ _____

_____

_____

_____

"We are confident, I say, and would prefer to be away from the body and at home with the Lord."

2 Corinthians 5:8

HALF PAST DON'T CARE

December

27 Does social media make you feel good or bad about yourself? Why?

20__ _____

_____

_____

_____

20__ _____

_____

_____

_____

20__ _____

_____

_____

_____

"Do not conform to the pattern of this world, but be transformed by the renewing of your mind. Then you will be able to test and approve what God's will is - his good, pleasing and perfect will."

Romans 12:2

December 28

What made you feel really good about yourself this week?

20__ _____
_____
_____
_____

20__ _____
_____
_____
_____

20__ _____
_____
_____
_____

"Fixing our eyes on Jesus, the pioneer and perfecter of faith."

Hebrews 12:2

December

29 What made you feel really bad about yourself this week?

20__ _____

_____

_____

_____

20__ _____

_____

_____

_____

20__ _____

_____

_____

_____

"Be alert and of sober mind. Your enemy the devil prowls around like a roaring lion looking for someone to devour."

1 Peter 5:8

December

30 What is one issue you've thought about this week that you need to release and move on?

20__ _____

_____

_____

_____

20__ _____

_____

_____

_____

20__ _____

_____

_____

_____

"Submit yourselves, then, to God."

James 4:7

December °°° 31

Draw a picture of your family ...

20__

20__

20__